from seed to apple

Inspirational stories from Washington's classrooms, featuring the Teachers, Principals, and Classified School Employees of the Year

VOLUME XI
2021

Disclaimer and Copyright Statement and Policy

This collection is a shout-out and Arsenio Hall fist pump to our communities and everyone who makes the world of public education magical — especially during this challenging time of a pandemic, our historic reckoning with racism, the devastating impacts of climate change, toilet paper shortages, murder hornets, failed sourdough starters, mask debates, round-the-clock Zoom meetings, and (possibly) the end of pants.

We hope that these interesting times will help us reimagine schools as places that provide equitable, authentic, and meaningful learning opportunities for all.

Table of Contents

AMY CAMPBELL

*2020 Washington State
Teacher of the Year*

Helen Baller Elementary School
Camas School District

Foreword

The year 2020 has taught me something of myself, but more importantly it has taught me something about other people and renewed my teacher "why."

Having spent the last 13 years of my career in a classroom, I can definitively tell you the best part of teaching is learning. While there was a point in my early career where I defined "professional learning" as the carefully crafted conferences and classes I took to collect clock hours, 2020 has been a stark reminder that some of the best reflective opportunities are gifted to us in the stories from our students and colleagues.

Shared personal experiences help us build our empathy and understanding of the diverse populations we serve. My ability to serve and create equitable opportunities for students is connected to my understanding of who they are and the experiences they bring.

This year's *From Seed to Apple* stories provide a robust picture of the diverse experiences of students and educators

Inspirational stories from Washington's classrooms, featuring the Teachers, Principals, and Classified School Employees of the Year

ix

in Washington. From the science classroom of a teacher offering her reflection on the power of extending grace to the remarkable perseverance of learning second languages at a variety of ages, each story in this book will open your heart and mind to what it means to teach, expand your capacity for supporting educators, and renew your hope in public education.

2020 has taught me a lot. The stories I have read and heard shape the way I now see this world beyond my own classroom. Stories, often hard to share, can be a gateway for people with different experiences to understand not just how to make change in this world, but why. What an honor to be able to offer you this collection, as a reminder that growth, change, and learning happen all the time — all around us. Our ability to see difference as an asset and extend empathy as needed will help us improve outcomes for students in Washington schools.

DEVIN BAUER

2021 Northeast ESD 101
Regional Teacher of the Year

Lakeside High School
Nine Mile Falls School District

High Expectations

It's their dream, not ours

What do you want to be when you grow up? It's the question every young person gets asked as they navigate adolescence. In adulthood, some of us are still trying to answer this question. Through my 12 years of teaching, I have heard every response from a volcanologist to an NFL superstar to anything in between. This one question answers many questions about someone's interests, personality, and personal preferences. As educators, it is imperative for us to ask this question and ask it often; this question helps us learn about students' hopes and dreams and allows us to better assist in their journey.

When we think of individuals described as naturals at their crafts, we picture success stories like Bill Gates and his way with computers or Russell Wilson and his ability to float a deep ball, dropping it into his receiver's hands like an infant being laid down for a nap. For me, when it came to school, natural was the last word being used to describe my

Inspirational stories from Washington's classrooms, featuring the Teachers, Principals, and Classified School Employees of the Year

1

academic ability. Starting in my elementary school years, I was a struggling reader. My mom and dad read to me every night like many parents do, but for some reason I didn't understand, I just struggled. One fateful night, when I was in third grade, my mom and dad attended a parent-teacher conference at my school. My parents sat down with my teacher and listened as the teacher gave their assessment on how I was doing in school. Something that the teacher said that made my parents, to put it lightly, very upset. The teacher had said, "I don't see your son going to college, but rather entering some sort of trade." As a young elementary school student, I had hopes, plans, and aspirations to work in the medical field, just like my dad. Thus, the upset response of my parents.

It turns out, I had a reading disability. Now I was lucky — my parents were in a position to be able to seek extra support for my reading disability, held me accountable for my schooling, and never let me forget: "We do what we have to do in order to do what we want to do." Trade schools are important, and fulfill the aspirations of some students, but it was not what I wanted to do. This teacher's expectations for my future did not match my own hopes. I feel fortunate to have had the support I did at home where my parents' expectations matched my own. I did not know about this until my mom told me after I graduated from Eastern Washington University with a bachelor's degree in teaching special education.

The start of the 2020 school year marked my 12th year as a high school special education teacher, and I can't see myself doing anything different. My students amaze me every day, but for many of them, like myself and Joey, school does not come naturally. Joey transferred in from another school his freshman year and was placed on my caseload. He had not had a lot of success at his previous school and had a failing grade in every class on his transcript. I knew the question to ask in our first meeting together:

"What do you want to do after you graduate from high school, Joey?"

This one question gives me much insight into their world, and for this young man, he wanted to play football in the NFL. I should tell you that in order to play in the NFL, you must first get accepted into college to play football. I must also point out that this young man was 6'4" and 200 pounds when standing on a one-foot box wrapped with a soaking wet towel. At that moment, I had a choice: take the wheel and steer this young man in a different direction or support him in his goal and get to work.

I realized the severity of this young man's struggle when he took his first basic art quiz. The quiz, like many quizzes we give students in school, consisted of matching 10 terms to their definitions — easy, right? On the first attempt Joey scored a two out of ten. The art teacher reached out to me and asked if I would help him study. After that he could retake the quiz. On his second attempt, after studying for thirty minutes with me, he scored a three out of ten. I had Joey make some flash cards and take them home to study. He came back the next day proud that he had studied that night and again in the morning with his grandma. He sat down to take the quiz and scored a two out of ten. At this point, I knew that we had some rough seas ahead and that

Inspirational stories from Washington's classrooms, featuring the Teachers, Principals, and Classified School Employees of the Year

3

we were going to have to work really hard to meet his goal.

As Joey navigated his way through high school, there were many ups and downs. There were also many other people who said he couldn't go to college because he wouldn't be successful without the support he was receiving in high school. What these people couldn't comprehend was Joey's internal drive and motivation to make his dream become a reality. We continued to work through difficult classes like Algebra II, Spanish, and Bio Tech. When Joey graduated from high school he had a 2.9 GPA and was accepted to Eastern Washington University. He was not playing football, but he was continuing his hard work to eventually get there. And get there he did.

I am happy to share that this young man finished his first year at Eastern Washington University with a 3.4 GPA and has since transferred to Whitworth University where he will be a student and a member of their football team. It is moments like these, whether we as educators are able to witness them or not, that make our career worthwhile.

Honoring students' dreams for themselves and holding them to high expectations is imperative to maximizing their potential and educational growth. This is exactly what was instilled in Joey: the belief that he could succeed. As educators it is important to remember that the students are the captains of their own ships, and it is our responsibility to support and help them as they navigate adolescence. When students have a say in their journey, they are both bought in and given the opportunity to reach their goals. It is the role of educators to encourage, offer suggestions at times, and occasionally catch them when they fall, all the while reminding them of their strength and potential. Through this process, students begin to build on their strengths and gain the confidence needed to tackle life even when they are faced with significant challenges. All students have strengths, and with support and guidance from adults, all students can reach their full potential. I lived that experience with supportive middle and high school teachers, as well as my parents. Joey, too, lived that experience.

Every day, I am reminded of the difference it made in my life to have someone believe in me, and I am passionate that my students know I believe in them and their dreams. I challenge educators to listen to your students; learn about their strengths, needs, and dreams; build relationships; and work with students to make their dreams become reality.

Inspirational stories from Washington's classrooms, featuring the Teachers, Principals, and Classified School Employees of the Year

5

"I quickly became very frustrated when I didn't immediately understand. But when she soon realized that I didn't get it, she put down her pencil, looked me dead in my eyes, and said, 'To succeed, you must be given a chance to fail.' I am reminded each day of her voice telling me that I could succeed because I was allowed to fail."

Isaac Yi
Reading Between the Lines

MEGAN ANDERSON REILLY
2021 ESD 105
Regional Teacher of the Year

AC Davis High School
Yakima School District

What Is Grace For?

How pandemic education could change what it means to meet students where they are

In the beginning of this pandemic school year, I felt like a giant inflatable duck, gliding smoothly across the water. This imagery comes from one of my favorite daily emotional check-ins in my Spanish class. The check-in includes nine images of enormous inflatable ducks with picture one being a giant, full of air, majestic rubber duck and picture nine being the same duck, but completely deflated. These pictures depict the range of pandemic emotions that I like to refer to as the "Corona Coaster." Picture one was my August duck—energetic, optimistic, and ready to defeat all obstacles that stood in my way. It didn't take long until one day in September, I hit a low point on the Corona Coaster and felt like duck number nine. In addition to the normal stresses of teaching virtually, the day included:

- Frantic texts between friends about the possibility that we had all been exposed to COVID-19.

- A message of sympathy from a parent, which said

Inspirational stories from Washington's classrooms, featuring the Teachers, Principals, and Classified School Employees of the Year

7

that during my class, she saw her daughter in bed, covers over her head, not paying attention. The mother looked at the computer and saw all 28 other students with their cameras off. She heard me asking questions, getting no response, and then me pleading "Anyone there? Anyone? Am I muted? Am I frozen?"

- An afternoon meeting with my administrator about my evaluation where I revealed that I would have little data to show student growth since I had so few students consistently engaging in online learning.

- The discovery that my own children had spent their school day on YouTube while eating multiple bags of microwave popcorn.

- The first presidential debate.

As I lay in bed that evening, I thought about my students at the large high school where I teach in Yakima and wondered where they were on their Corona Coaster. Did something good happen to make them feel successful, productive, and happy? Or, is something heavy on their minds and hearts? I wondered how the national spotlight on racism was affecting my students, 90% of whom are students of color. I wondered about the impact the increased unemployment has had on their families, especially since 80% were identified as low-income pre-pandemic. I wondered about students' current health and feeling of safety given we were a national hotspot for COVID-19 for most of the summer. I started thinking about the many students who were failing my class, which led me to think about the many students I am failing as a teacher. The current reality weighed heavy on my chest.

Since schools closed in March, the concept of "giving grace" has been a common theme in discussions about education. Educators have been encouraged to give grace to our peers, to ourselves, to our administrators, and to our students. In the beginning, "grace" was described as forgiveness and letting go of expectations of perfection; trying, failing, and trying again. Grace also included a "do no harm" grading policy. This policy eliminated the possibility of students failing and prevented grades from going down from March 17. Grace allowed time for districts to get computers out to students and find solutions to internet access. Grace gave educators time to get resources, learn digital platforms, and discover effective teaching in a virtual environment. Grace gave students a chance to learn the system, figure out what virtual learning was all about, and find tools and strategies that worked for them. All this problem-solving and learning was happening without the stress of grades and with an understanding that we were in an emergency. This situation was new for everyone, and we all needed time and patience to adapt.

Now, we have had months of continued school shutdowns, reinstated grading policies, and refined virtual instruction. While many districts have helped solve issues of internet and computer access, others are still working to address this need. Teachers are familiar with virtual instruction; some are excited by the new technology and others feel overwhelmed. Students have been taught virtual learning expectations. At the same time, it is evident that many of my students are still facing substantial and complex challenges. So, what does grace look like now?

Inspirational stories from Washington's classrooms, featuring the Teachers, Principals, and Classified School Employees of the Year

9

This focus on giving grace reminded me of my first year teaching. In particular, the impact that misplaced grace had on four amazing, hard-working students. They had started school in the United States two years prior. In their home countries, they had experienced interrupted formal education. It was obvious that they had gaps in their academic skills due to missed school. In addition, they were still at the beginning stages of communicating effectively in English. However, since these students were willing learners who took advantage of every educational opportunity, teachers — including myself — gave them a grade based on effort, not mastery. A grade based on grace. As a result, these students were awarded full-ride scholarships to universities. "What a celebration!" I thought. "A true success story."

A year later, one of these four students visited me. Thrilled, I asked him how school was going and what it was like. He told me that he, along with the other three students, were no longer in college; they had to drop out. Due to their academic skill level, they had been assigned remedial classes that their scholarships did not pay for. They said that the remedial classes they had to take were too hard and it became too expensive to continue.

I gave my students what I thought was grace years ago, and I allowed it to overshadow my responsibility to ensure my students graduate from school with the ability to make their own choices about their future. Right now, we have many students who, like these four students, are experiencing interrupted formal education. In addition, they are at a low point on the Corona Coaster. They are unable to meaningfully engage in distance learning. What started out as weeks of online learning has turned into months and possibly at least a year. The effect of this disruption will vary by student, but it has the potential to reach beyond grades and into students' future opportunities.

While I had issued too much grace in grading those four students, I came to the realization that other parts of our system did not offer enough. The systems that incentivize and penalize on-time graduation rates did not translate into what would have been best for my students: more time in high school. The well-intentioned and generous scholarships prevented students from using their funds to take required classes could have issued more grace. In addition, the colleges and universities could have offered more grace by finding ways for students to access core classes with support, especially given that the impact of remedial classes in colleges and universities is questionable at best. These same realities will impact current students, especially those in high school. The number of students who will experience challenges due to interrupted education has significantly increased.

The day after my Corona Coaster low, I turned on my computer to start another virtual school day. I checked my email and was relieved to see a message from Tomás, a student I had not heard from for weeks. He had been in Mexico with his grandmother since the start of the semester. In his email, he apologized for not doing his assignments for my class due to limited access to the internet. I wrote back to Tomás some alternative assignment options based on what we had been learning in class. Maybe instead

Inspirational stories from Washington's classrooms, featuring the Teachers, Principals, and Classified School Employees of the Year

11

of completing daily assignments, he could write some questions and record an interview with his grandmother or another family member. Or perhaps he could journal about some of the daily activities and things that he likes and does not like about where he is. I let him know that he could still demonstrate his learning in a different way. Grace.

I have many students who, like Tomás, can't keep up with assignments for all kinds of valid reasons. Teaching during this pandemic has forced me to be more flexible about their learning — adopting grading practices that allow for alternative assignments, extending deadlines, giving multiple opportunities, and allowing retakes. And while this flexibility can be challenging, it is also exciting because it makes sure that fewer students are left behind.

My new understanding of grace involves flexibility, responsiveness, and accountability to learning. I hope that broader systems also find ways to issue this same grace. Are we willing to get rid of the stigma and the penalties associated with giving students an additional year of school if that is something that would benefit them? Can we create more alternative pathways for students based on need? Are school districts, universities, and colleges able to collaborate to redesign student supports that are more effective and inclusive? How can we encourage organizations that provide scholarships to be flexible?

We cannot fully control the ups and downs on the Corona Coaster. At the same time, with the right application of grace, we can influence how students feel about school and keep at least a little air in their duck till the end of this.

And we can ensure that this application of grace survives this pandemic to positively impact our students' futures.

Inspirational stories from Washington's classrooms, featuring the Teachers, Principals, and Classified School Employees of the Year

13

"Winning is different for everyone. From taking first place in an event to learning a skill for improving the quality of life — both are meaningful. Knowing what winning looks like for a student means really getting to know that student and what they are good at. Relationships like that take time to build."

Katie Lee
Determined to Win

ERIN LARK
2021 ESD 112
Regional Teacher of the Year

iTech Preparatory School
Vancouver Public Schools

Forgiveness for the Frogs

Sometimes the things that matter most are the small moments we almost forget

You never plan to cry in front of your students, but there I was, tears streaming down my face on a perfectly pleasant autumn afternoon.

Teaching surprises me every day. I research, prepare, and deliver, yet constant adjustments are commonplace in my world because even the best-laid plans need to fit a variety of very unique circumstances that can't ever fully be predicted. When you bring together a group of people for learning, you have to make room for the lessons that will actually shake out, not just those you intended.

Autumn in Vancouver can roll out like a movie set; leaves awash in sunset shades with just the right amount of swirling around one's boots while walking to school. Students with backpacks and ruddy cheeks cheerfully fill the halls with an ease of chatter that comes with October territory. The newness of the school year has sloughed off and made way for readiness and routines. We have buckled

Inspirational stories from Washington's classrooms, featuring the Teachers, Principals, and Classified School Employees of the Year

15

into the business of learning.

Third period students had tumbled into the classroom after lunch, dutifully taken out their science notebooks, and engaged in discussion about the restoration of the Mt. St. Helens landscape after the 1980 eruption. We read through statistics estimating the quantity and variety of animals lost and pored over pictures of blackened earth stripped of its trees, their charred branches and limbs found in haphazard piles downstream from the blast. Students had just learned lahars (destructive volcanic mudflows) are no joke. Thus far, all had gone as planned.

The classroom door opened, just as I'd paused some video footage of a massive and unstoppable tide of mud and flaming debris that wiped out a valley of lifeforms in a matter of minutes. The students and I blinked at the sudden intrusion of photons and an unexpected visitor. The unidentifiable person stood framed in the doorway, sunlight streaming around them into the darkened room, instantly intriguing all current classroom occupants.

"Hi," I said, not recognizing the silhouette. "Can I help you?"

"You are really hard to find," he said, stepping forward and taking off his hat.

One of my current students helpfully flipped on the lights to reveal a uniformed young man with a signed visitor badge in one hand. I am fairly certain I squinted for a moment, my teacher brain digging through the stacks of my ever-expanding backlog of faces and names. I began walking forward, thinking I would better understand the situation after introductions when I saw the nametag. MICHAELS, it read, and I stopped.

My students had been uncharacteristically silent in their seats. Their eyes volleyed between their suddenly speechless teacher in the middle of the room and the stranger who'd just entered at the back, brushing an errant leaf off the crisp black wool on his shoulder. They waited for direction, explanation, or guidance as to what — or rather who — had brought science to an abrupt halt.

"You moved schools," he said, smiling. "I asked for you there and they told me you are here now."

"It is so good to see you!" I responded, saying what I think any teacher in this situation would, desperate for a first name to surface from the depths. "I can tell you have been busy," I added, weakly gesturing to the uniform, buying time for a nugget of recollection.

"Yeah," he replied, shrugging a bit, "I just came back from training a few months ago and I'm shipping out soon. I wanted to stop by and see my teachers before..."

His voice trailed off while the unsaid description of risk an overseas deployment would mean that year hung in the air between us.

Wanting to keep the mood light, I started, "Class, this is one of my former students..." I turned toward them and he picked up the slack for me, rotating to see everyone.

"Michaels," he smiled at the class, Private Michaels," he smiled at the class. "But call me Skyler."

Inspirational stories from Washington's classrooms, featuring the Teachers, Principals, and Classified School Employees of the Year

17

Like a cinematic flashback, snippets of the past came forward in a series of scenes of a quiet, yet affable redhead from a class some handful of years ago. I remembered his face, the younger version, but struggled to recall much else.

He continued, with the rapt attention of thirty teens. "Your teacher is a big reason I'm where I'm now. If she hadn't believed in me, pushed me to do something with myself, I wouldn't be where I am. You've got to listen to her."

My current charges turned to look at me with new reverence. This was a person who commanded respect, one of their own who'd made it out only to return and let them know they had something special going on. I wasn't altogether sure I deserved this attention.

"And," he continued conspiratorially, "she wasn't too hard on me when I didn't listen at first. Remember the time with the frogs?"

Oh yes, the frogs. I immediately recalled that class with Skyer and his friends. While I greeted students at the door one morning, a few early entrants quickly rearranged the deceased amphibians, prepped respectfully for that day's lab, into an ersatz conga line on a dissection tray. That group of friends had made for a fun and generally harmless (except to frogs) pack of dedicated learners. "That was the last time I ran dissections, you know," my smile betraying an attempt to look irritated.

Skyler spoke up and brought me back to the present.

"Well, it's late," he acknowledged, looking at his watch. "I didn't know I'd have an extra stop to say hello." I felt the nostalgic warmth begin to slip away, like a cat slinking out of a room in your peripheral vision. "I have to go," he apologized to all of us, "but thank you for letting me come by."

No, thank you, I thought, not wanting to let go of the past I had just found. I had been given a gift, just then, and this was only now starting to sink in. "Anytime," is what I said aloud, "please, keep in touch."

"Of course," he nodded, one hand opening the door while the other replaced the hat on his head. He paused to conclude, "and thank you, I mean it." The door closed behind Skyler Michaels and he was gone.

Cue tears.

I would like to be able to share that I discontinued the rest of science that day in order to reminisce with my students about our most cherished teachers, talk about their plans for the future, and what it meant to me to have a former student take the time to come back and tell me how it all turned out. I would like to be able to say I saw Skyler again and that I know he returned safely from serving his country.

Instead, I reached for a tissue to dab fervently at my eyes and attempted to salvage what was left of the class period. Perhaps foolishly, I did not take the opportunity to tell my students what they mean to us, how even if we forget some names, our wishes for their triumph are both wanted and needed in the world. I may not have told them this, but looking back, I think it was written on my face, during that deep breath I took before returning to our class.

Inspirational stories from Washington's classrooms, featuring the Teachers, Principals, and Classified School Employees of the Year

19

On the hard days, I question if my efforts have a lasting difference. Other days, I trust my abilities to make the right choices that move students forward. The thing is, students are watching and learning from me, from all of us, every day. Our role in their lives means more than we will ever realize.

Always, always extend forgiveness for the frogs.

DAVID BUITENVELD
2021 Capital Region ESD 113
Regional Teacher of the Year
Nisqually Middle School
North Thurston Public Schools

Remembering the Pandemic

Or, how we learned to stop worrying and changed education

"Mr. B, tell us about the pandemic."

There is at least one student in each class that asks some form of this question, and though it seems like they are asking about science, or maybe even about math, I understand what they are really asking. And so I begin: Once upon a time, things were different...

Our class is a group of 7th and 8th graders studying advanced mathematics. Although it is early in the semester, I already have good relationships with these students because I have been part of their journey. I was part of the team that began working with them in 5th grade to help them prepare for middle school. I also have a student teacher this year, Lisa, and although I have mentored new teachers before, it is particularly exciting for me because Lisa is a former student of mine.

To help my students understand the pandemic, I first ask

Inspirational stories from Washington's classrooms, featuring the Teachers, Principals, and Classified School Employees of the Year

21

them what they think education is for. Many students raise their hands, and this makes me smile, because I want students to have a sense of why they are here. Ella cares deeply about the environment and says that she is here to learn about climate and ecology so that she can become an environmental scientist and activist. Zander, our school DJ, is drumming lightly on his lap as his hand shoots up. He is passionate about creating music and tells us he is here to learn how to use technology to communicate with his community. Kyra has already been planning her run for ASB president and explains that she wants to learn about everything so she can be an effective leader. Interestingly, not one student said they were here because they have to be. And curiously, no one said they were here to learn math.

I next ask my students to think about why they are in this class. I am curious what students think about the role of math class in their lives, and also, how they came to be in an advanced math class. Our advanced math program is open to all students, even if they were previously enrolled in a math support class — students and families choose to be in this class. Daron, a 7th grader, shares his interest in engineering and his excitement about more challenges than he had in core math last year. Haley, an 8th grader, never felt "smart" at math and chose our math-empowerment support class in 6th grade. At the end of last year, she emailed to thank me for helping her see her hard work turn into confidence, and that she was choosing to try advanced math this year. She brims with quiet confidence as she tells the class about her journey.

Finally, I ask them what they think my job as a teacher should be. I wondered if this question would stump them, but again the hands shoot up. Isaac says he remembers when I visited his class in 5th grade and told them that middle school was where they decided the kind of person they were going to grow up to become — maybe that is what a teacher's job is. Haley jumps in again and says that a teacher's job is to show students that however smart they think they are or not, students can learn anything they want. Elise has been pondering and slowly raises her hand. She explains that she wants to live a good life and make a difference in the world, and that she thinks I should help with this.

This is a good time to hear from Lisa, our student teacher, so I ask her to describe what it was like when she was in school.

She begins, "When I was your age, my friends and I felt like we were in school either because we had to be, or because it would lead to a job with a high salary someday."

She shares that the most important things were getting good grades and high test scores so you could get into advanced classes. She says that the things that she was most passionate about, the things that were most important to her, were explored outside of class.

Lisa pauses for a moment, staring off into space, then says, "I remember how stressed out my friends and I felt the week of state testing... it's hard to describe how much pressure we felt, and I am so glad it is different for you all." "

And the teachers felt it too," she says, glancing at me and laughing. "Even Mr. B seemed to drink more coffee

Inspirational stories from Washington's classrooms, featuring the Teachers, Principals, and Classified School Employees of the Year

23

during testing."

Lisa was my student during the COVID pandemic. She paints a picture of math class, and of school in general, as divorced from students' lives and aspirations—a picture of school in which educational priorities were driven by accountability to high-stakes testing and data.

"Did you know," I ask them, "that we used to put you in advanced math based on test scores?"

This gives them pause. "You mean we couldn't choose to be here?" asks Haley.

"What if we just had a bad day for the test?" exclaims Ella.

Today we understand that accountability must be driven by educational priorities and the things we most value: students attending to their own well-being; students developing the skills and confidence to learn anything they choose, over the course of their entire lives; and academic content connecting to students' lives and communities, and to the larger world, across domains, in service of discovering and pursuing purposeful lives.

Once upon a time, things were different. It has been eight years since the COVID pandemic of 2020 and the effects on schools were so disruptive that a critical mass of educators, administrators, politicians, and families began having conversations about the fundamental priorities, assumptions, and equities in our schools and forced us to create a new paradigm. Though in the middle of a traumatic experience, these people bravely resisted the forces pulling us backwards toward the familiar but flawed. Lisa is part of a new wave of young educators who experienced the pandemic as students and participated in the transformations that occurred as a result. And those of us who taught before and during those changing times experienced a renewal of our sense of purpose, and we remembered why we became teachers.

Inspirational stories from Washington's classrooms, featuring the Teachers, Principals, and Classified School Employees of the Year

25

"We look for joy in the unlikeliest places — and then we share it with one another. Hearing their joy sparks it in me. Landing their first job. Spending time with a friend socially distanced. Getting accepted into college. So many things to celebrate.

But there are also days when joy seems elusive."

Brooke Brown
Shifting Perspectives

DAVID COOKE
2020 Washington State
Secondary Principal of the Year

Jemtegaard Middle School
Washougal School District

The World I Could Not See

A home visit redefines a principal's practice

My first day at high school in 1996 was daunting. I opened the door and saw many students packed into a tight hallway. There were holes in the ceiling where water dripped out into the trash cans below. Teachers were tightly navigating through the body of students trying to get to class. As I walked down the hall, I bumped into some football players in letterman jackets. I said to a teacher as I tried to catch my breath, "These are the biggest seniors I have ever seen." The teacher looked at me and said, "This is the sophomore hall." And so began my first day as a teacher in the American education system.

While I did not grow up in the American school system, I had many advantages that helped me navigate my new environment. I could speak English, and the American and Australian school systems had many similarities, so my training in Australia helped me transition quickly. A bonus for me was that I came from a country that was seen as positive and intriguing to the people that I worked with. I

Inspirational stories from Washington's classrooms, featuring the Teachers, Principals, and Classified School Employees of the Year

27

was deemed as a safe newcomer. Nobody felt threatened by the Aussie. I never felt unwanted. It was easy for me to assimilate into American culture and be accepted. I understood the school system. It worked for me, and I worked hard to maintain it for the good of all students. Eventually, I would be the primary keeper of the educational system as a middle school principal.

I prided myself on listening to students, being flexible when I needed to, and giving students chances to redeem themselves. However, as a principal, there would come a point when students who would not change their behavior and follow the system I had created would have to be removed. I had to do what I believed was in the best interest of the student body. I told myself, "Of course the student would understand why as I was more than fair." So would the parents. After all, I was being flexible and understanding. Their child had multiple chances to fix their behavior, and they didn't, so I had to take action. Suspending students was not what I wanted to do, but it was a necessary evil in order to keep the whole educational system going.

In 2006, in my third year of being a principal, I found that most students would generally following the expectations. The system was working well. A majority of people were happy, and there was no need to change. Those who did not knew what would happen.

Then a new sixth grader turned up who was not doing what was expected. Manny was getting involved in fights with other students. He was making other students unsafe. I had tried my firm-but-fair bag of tricks, but Manny would not change his behavior. An incredibly likable young man with the most memorable smile you would ever see, I thought that he was manipulating me in order to avoid being punished. After the third fighting incident, I was ready to long-term suspend him. After all, he had been warned. I had tried to call his parents, but they did not respond. An example had to be made to show all students that the rules must be followed. I am not sure if it was that smile or the fact that Manny made me laugh, but I decided for the first time as a principal to do a house call. Manny had to conform to the expectations. I would tell Mom, through a translator, that he had to change, or he would not be at my school.

On a cold October morning, I drove out to the berry farm where Manny and his family lived. My team included my administrative intern Katie and a Spanish-speaking parent, Sarah. We entered the farm and walked towards a small house near a large machinery shed. I was confused as Sarah walked right past the house. I asked why we weren't going in and she said that Manny's family did not live here. Manny's family lived in the machinery shed. I walked into the shed, which had been converted into six separate apartments. Each apartment, which had a number on each door, was about the size of a standard living room. Two large lamps hung at the top of the shed, providing the only light once the sun went down. The floors were all concrete. The only furniture that I could see in this large shed was a brown couch covered in dust. This was where our meeting would be held.

Manny's mother Benita and brother, Ramiro, came out to greet us. Benita quickly brushed the dirt off the couch so

Inspirational stories from Washington's classrooms, featuring the Teachers, Principals, and Classified School Employees of the Year

29

that we could sit down and sat on a metal chair alongside Ramiro. Manny was not at the meeting because he was at school. For the first time in my career, I was involved in a trilingual conversation. Benita did not speak Spanish. She spoke an indigenous Mexican language, so she spoke to Ramiro. Ramiro did not speak English, so he spoke to Sarah. Katie and I could not speak either Spanish or the indigenous language, so we were totally reliant on Sarah.

The fork of the road in my educational career started in that gray, gloomy shed. My first thoughts were questions: How could anyone live here? How cold must it be at night? How could anybody concentrate here? What other supplies did they need just to get through the day? How can you do homework without a real home?

When I sat down to talk to Benita, I felt a great sense of pity. And then Benita spoke. She told us about her journey to get her family to the United States for a better life. Benita and Ramiro had worked on this farm since they had arrived six months earlier. Benita told us how her husband had been deported. As she spoke about her five children, it was clear that she had so many hopes and dreams for her children and wanted them to thrive in this new environment. Benita was not happy with Manny's behavior and still wanted accountability for his behavior. But she also wanted him to get the support that would give him a chance. She was grateful that we came to visit. My meeting was supposed to be focused on what Manny was doing wrong, but it became clear to me that it wasn't just Manny who was not meeting expectations. I had just met one of the most courageous and inspirational people in my life.

I left the farm changed forever.

The revelation that hit me at the berry farm was clear: I had built a school system that worked well for me. It appealed to my values, my ideas of education, and my experiences. For many people in the community I served, my system worked. However, for many it did not give them the support they needed to be successful. That had to change. I thought about my first experience in an American school and how overwhelmed I was as an adult. How must it look for a tiny sixth grade student who had been in the country for less than six months? Where would he even start to try to navigate his new educational world?

While I was an immigrant myself, my experiences were completely different from a student who spoke limited English or Spanish, had minimal education, and knew nothing of how American school systems worked. My bias and assumptions were that students who came from Spanish-speaking countries were not successful because of the language barrier. By saying that, I had essentially told them that it was their problem and they had to adjust in order to be successful. In fact, it was my system that had to adjust. This was not a language issue. It was an access issue, and I held the keys to the access.

My biggest problem was that I was not educated in methods to systematically change a system to support students like Manny. I had to get myself a consultant and there was only one candidate for the job: Manny. I interviewed Manny about helping me and we quickly came to 'terms.' We would meet every two weeks, eat a Hershey chocolate bar, and chat about how he was doing. This was our arrangement for the next three years.

Manny became my greatest teacher. He was my window into a world that I could not see. He helped me see the many hurdles that came his way. So many school doors were closed for him and his family. Items that I took for granted such as food, school supplies, and technology were a daily struggle for Manny. Manny did not know how to ask for this help. Instead of getting to know him, my staff and I reminded Manny on a regular basis that he had to conform to the current system by punishing him.

We punished Manny with his grades for not completing his homework, even though it was difficult for him to study with so much noise in a densely populated shed and limited light at night. He also helped his younger siblings when he got home. The role models in his life had less education than he had and could not help him, despite their desire to. Teachers also did not have the capacity to reach out to families like Manny's because the district did not have a Spanish-speaking point person. Manny talked about how frustrated he was that other students did not treat him well because of his Latinx identity, so he would lash out. Nobody heard his side; we only looked at his actions. The question changed from, 'Why is Manny failing?' to 'Why wouldn't he fail?'

Manny and I, with the support of staff, began turning around our system to meet the needs of our Latinx students. Manny taught me to never assume. When I implemented a plan at my school, I would ask Manny what he thought. I would think about how this would be accessed by the people living in the apartments at the berry farm. I thought about the lack of staff that a family like Manny's could even talk to. I began meeting with my Latinx families, gathering as much information as I could, and often leaving with more questions than answers. I was always the student in these meetings.

Manny became a beloved student at our school. Many of his great qualities that I had ignored shone through. He went on to high school and graduated even after he was diagnosed with a learning disability. As for me, I have continued my quest since this meeting 10 years ago to change our educational system so that all students can navigate it well. As educators, we should never assume that our system is straightforward for our families. We have to keep asking questions, building partnerships, and growing together. For me, this approach has led to a growing partnership where trust has been built and barriers continue to come down. Thank you, Manny.

Inspirational stories from Washington's classrooms, featuring the Teachers, Principals, and Classified School Employees of the Year

33

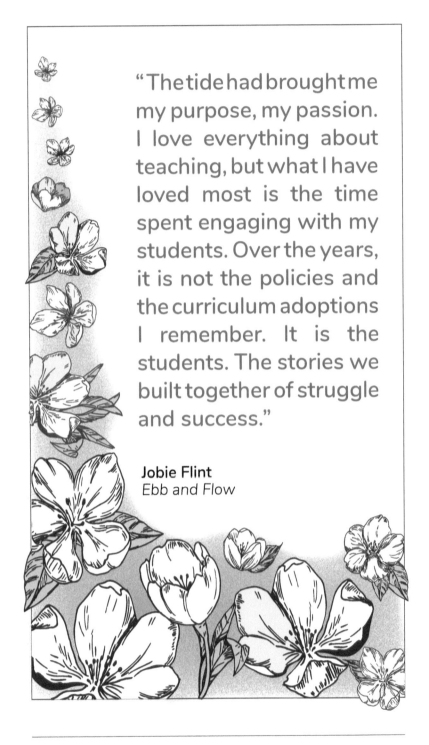

"The tide had brought me my purpose, my passion. I love everything about teaching, but what I have loved most is the time spent engaging with my students. Over the years, it is not the policies and the curriculum adoptions I remember. It is the students. The stories we built together of struggle and success."

Jobie Flint
Ebb and Flow

DAVID TRACEWELL
2021 Olympic Region ESD 114 Regional Teacher of the Year
Central Kitsap High School
Central Kitsap School District

Gloria Gaynor's Favorite Son

One kid's courage to be different shapes a teacher's practice

Fourth grade. Ms. Deschamp's, Room 4-A. Gary Underwood is who I remember most, besides Sarah who always wore those big doofy loop earrings. Always, until she got one of them caught on one of the coat rack hooks as she was running out to recess. YANK! She kept running while the loop earring made continuous rotations on that hook. I don't remember them ever finding the rest of her earlobe.

But, Gary Underwood. He was that one student who stuck out. Gary Underwood, always diggin' his nose in class, unabashedly. Gary Underwood, who we used to call Gary Underwear (such an obvious insult, I don't know why we ever laughed at it), would never get mad. He was too busy being different.

Gary marched to the beat of his own drum, cliché as that may sound. He always wore Toughskins, those brown and red socks from a certain Washington, DC football team, and

Inspirational stories from Washington's classrooms, featuring the Teachers, Principals, and Classified School Employees of the Year

35

one of those baseball jerseys with the dorky in-between length sleeves. You know, the jersey that was all white except for the sleeves. Well Gary had five of those jerseys, and each jersey had a different colored sleeve. Some of the girls had a tally sheet where they checked off which color jersey Gary wore. It's like they wanted to figure him out. How does he mix up his wardrobe? Girls can be as mean as boys.

But the icing on the cake was the iron-on he had on those jerseys. Every one of those jerseys had the same iron-on: The Incredible Hulk. And I knew where he got those iron-ons. It was on the back of Fruity Pebbles cereal. His family must have been one Fruity Pebbles eatin' bunch, 'cause you had to save up at least two or three proofs of purchase for each. I personally didn't like Fruity Pebbles, 'cause my Dad used to joke that Fruity Pebbles wasn't actually cereal, but really Fred's daughter all chopped up. That's why they named the cereal after her. He told my brother and me this when I was in second grade and even though I stopped believing him in third, I actually discovered that I didn't like Fruity Pebbles. They got soggy too fast.

But what I remember most about Gary is his intensity. He had this "I'm not crazy, everyone else is" look that you just couldn't get over. I mean, it was hard to like the guy 'cause he was so creepy at times. And that intensity, combined with his willingness to be different, etched one of the funniest moments I have from my childhood into my memory.

We were at recess playing dodgeball. Almost all of the boys in the class were playing, including Gary, and some

From Seed to Apple

fifth graders from Mr. Meachum's class. Gary was always chosen last for teams. I mean, he's even at the bottom of the list alphabetically in every class. It's like God purposely put him there. Well anyway, you know how dodgeball is played. It's like a legal way of hitting other students, except with a big, red rubber ball. And back then we always played with the rule that you could hit anywhere. I remember Gary finally getting into the ring. Every one of us wanted to be the one to smack him with the ball — even his own teammates.

Gary was always competitive, but not with others — with himself. He wouldn't just jump into the ring like the rest of us. He's psyche himself up first. I can still see Gary runnin' around the ring, fists balled, teeth clenched. In my mind he's still squeezing his fists so hard he's shaking. Then he'd dance.

Gary Underwood, with his Toughskins, bright socks, and mail-in Incredible Hulk iron-on jersey shirts, doing a little jig around the ring — so intense. All wrapped up and consumed in his little world. And then to top it off, he'd start yelling, "I WILL SURVIVE! I WILL SURVIVE!" The disco anthem of the Seventies being replayed in the mind of Gary Underwood — Hulkamaniac.

"At first I was afraid...I was petrified...I WILL SURVIVE!" Everybody would start laughin' and pointin' at Gary, the one-man disco machine. "Go...walk out that door...Just turn around now...you're not welcome anymore..."

"Shatap, you idiot! Get in the ring!"

"As long as I know how to love...I WILL SURVIVE!"

Inspirational stories from Washington's classrooms, featuring the Teachers, Principals, and Classified School Employees of the Year

37

Gary jumped in the ring, still doing his dance, and yelling his intense little white butt off. And before he knew it, SMACK! Right in the kisser! I beamed that ball right into his face. There was no survivin' today. Boy, the high I got from that one blow was so intense. I felt like I had won the Superbowl of dodgeball. I thought I knew what Roger Staubach felt after winning the Superbowl in his third year. Gloria Gaynor would have been proud to see me knock Gary, I thought. He wasn't doin' any justice to the song.

Twenty-fifth grade. Mr. Tracewell's, Room 1204, and I am ashamed that I did not become Gary's friend. Given the opportunity, I chose the crowd over lending a hand. I know now that Gary probably would have been the most loyal friend ever. What have I learned since then from Gary? Well, for one, I have five pairs of the same comfortable Eddie Bauer pants that I wear throughout the work week. Gary knew what he liked: baseball and the Incredible Hulk. How cool is that? And he knew how to be comfortable in his own skin, even at age nine.

I've also learned to be competitive with myself. I adopted this attitude especially in college because I was paying for it. To be intrinsically motivated towards success. And I have learned to live fearlessly through my mistakes. Like Gary, I sing out loud with the headphones on during my walks even though I can't sing and may embarrass myself when others are around. My kids hate when I do that while waiting for them during their sports practices.

Now, in my classroom, no proverbial dodge balls are thrown. And if one does get loose, I am there to intercept it.

The only dodge balls thrown are by me at me as I use self-deprecating humor at times to draw my students' attention, and they can laugh at my expense. I share this story at the beginning of every year to show my students who I was and how people can change. I share my regrets and shame. And I remind them that my classroom is a safe place where we make room for all the Garys of the world.

"Mr. Tracewell. There's no one named Gary. Parents don't name their kids Gary anymore."

"I know. There aren't any Barbaras, Richards, and Cindys either, but it's our job to look out for them in case they do show up and anyone else for that matter."

"Oh, okay. Oh, I get it. And we're not really throwing dodgeballs in here, right?"

"You got it."

Inspirational stories from Washington's classrooms, featuring the Teachers, Principals, and Classified School Employees of the Year

39

"My best wasn't good enough at the time, and I couldn't see beyond my pride and insecurity to tell him that. One of the takeaways from living through a pandemic is that we can finally drop the pretense that we're 'fine,' that everything is 'good' because, well, we're not and it's not."

Ben Ballew
(Not) Crying in Petco

BROOKE BROWN
2021 Washington State Teacher of the Year

Washington High School
Franklin Pierce School District

Shifting Perspectives

Balancing grief and joy is both the path through a pandemic and the key to lasting change

We all deserve an award for making it through 2020. So many parents and caregivers are working from home and doubling as teachers to their children. The sacrifices have been many and great. I can relate. We have four children. Balancing work and kids is difficult on the easiest of days. Showing up and trying to minimize trauma for all involved takes a lot of intentionality, grace and … coffee.

A few weeks ago, while I was recording a class session, my daughter walked behind me just out of the shower in her towel. Despite making the video unusable, it made me laugh. This is our new normal, and we are all doing the best we can. I now have a curtain rod running through my living room to provide some privacy and color to my background. We do what it takes to make the best of what we have. In addition to a curtain in the middle of our living room, my community and the connections I have with so many

Inspirational stories from Washington's classrooms, featuring the Teachers, Principals, and Classified School Employees of the Year

41

amazing people are getting me through this year.

I aim to model this in my remote instruction. When my students show up in my Zoom classroom, this is how we start; class begins in the chat box.

Does pineapple belong on pizza?

"Absolutely!"

"No way!"

"Only as long as there's jalapeños with it."

How are you today on a scale of 1–10?

"8 — I'm having a great day."

"3 — I'm tired of going to funerals. Covid sucks."

"Sorry I'm late, my WiFi was down this morning. How are you? What are we doing?"

While we have been mandated to physically distance, we must be intentional to connect socially — both as teachers and people. I connect with a colleague each morning to see how she has found joy the previous day and to share mine. This habit keeps me accountable. I have to look for joy, because I know I will have to share it daily. This is something I do in my class on a weekly basis as well. We look for joy in the unlikeliest places — and then we share it with one another. Hearing their joy sparks it in me. Landing their first job. Spending time with a friend socially distanced. Getting accepted into college. So many things to celebrate.

But there are also days when joy seems elusive.

We must show up on those days too. I read somewhere we are all in the same storm, but not in the same boat. We are all struggling in this pandemic in different ways: mental health, food insecurity, losing loved ones, feeling alone and isolated. We share those feelings in our virtual classroom too. Zoom doesn't stop us from creating an authentic classroom environment, intentionally building community, and increasing our social-emotional awareness to help navigate those storms.

COVID-19 has shifted the realities for so many of us. During the closure last spring, I read an article that helped to name what we were all going through — grief. Overnight, the seniors I teach lost spring sports, prom, and graduation. They were crushed. I have a 12th grade daughter who is navigating grief and loss this school year. Everything she has looked forward to is different. Will there be a soccer season? She's been team captain the last two years. Will there be assemblies? She's vice president of the student body. Will she get to be in the school's musical? Shrek was cancelled last spring. She misses her friends and teachers just as I miss my students and colleagues.

2020 has been a season of grief and joy. We need to understand and embrace both to make it through. There is a divide in this country that can seem insurmountable. The pandemic, the west coast on fire, the murder of George Floyd this summer — everything seemed to be spiraling out of control. The world felt like it was upside down.

To add to all the uncertainty (and homemade bread), I was pregnant in the middle of a pandemic.

Inspirational stories from Washington's classrooms, featuring the Teachers, Principals, and Classified School Employees of the Year

43

I delivered our beautiful son late in the night on a Thursday in July. He let out a loud cry, and — behind a mask — I shed tears of joy. He was healthy. Beautiful. Just what we never knew we were missing. Born at 36 weeks, he was a little premature but spent no time in the NICU. We would find out later that he has an extra chromosome — Trisomy 21. I didn't know what to do. I was lost. The grief for the life I had imagined for my son was overwhelming.

But I realized, over time, that there was joy too. We just have to keep searching for it. There was joy to be found in the many people in our community who lifted us up. People that we had poured into were now pouring into us. Friends we had supported during their tough seasons were showing up for ours. Dinners were delivered, gifts were dropped off. But the most important thing people gave us was their presence. They showed up. To show me, to show us that they cared. They sat with me, socially distanced, and listened. Sometimes no words were exchanged. There were phone calls, video chats, text messages. People shared space. Their presence was the best present because it helped us process the grief, so we could see the joy. Our son has the best smile, sleeps through the night, and gives the best snuggles. He brings so much joy to our lives and the lives of those around us.

When our circumstances are outside of our control, we must shift our perspective. We cannot shrink and step back. We must make space for grief and acknowledge its presence so we can continue to show up and search for joy. We must dry our tears and get back to life. Community and connection are what will get us through this pandemic. We need one another.

This is what drives me to show up for my students. For my colleagues. For my children. For myself. Before the pandemic, showing up meant taking the bus to school with your friends, going to class and participating in extracurriculars. Showing up virtually means partnering with our students and creating brave, authentic spaces for them to feel seen and heard, spaces where we can learn to have difficult conversations about systemic racism, climate change, the virus, and the uncertainty all around us. Deep breathing techniques, consistent check-ins, and space for conversation to flow help us to focus on what's really important: honoring and paying close attention to what students choose to share, inviting them into learning opportunities to help them process their own grief and joy.

We must continue to shift our perspectives in spite of our grief toward joy and understand that we are the answer we have been looking for. I'm not advocating for us to just forget and move on. We must hold the memory of grief so that we remain uncomfortable and unwilling to settle for going back to "normal." Change can be scary and unsettling, necessary and joyful. This is the time to embrace the "and." We must commit to showing up, for ourselves, our loved ones, and our community. Posting and talking about change won't create the more just world our future needs. We must put one foot in front of the other and do it even if we're afraid. Our communities are waiting for us to show up. Will you join me?

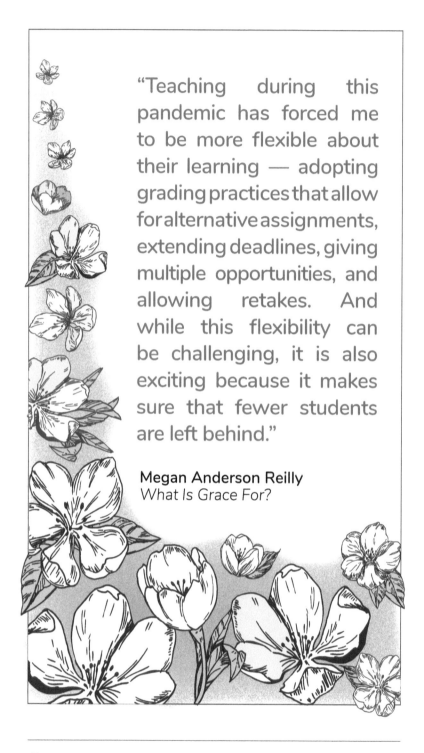

"Teaching during this pandemic has forced me to be more flexible about their learning — adopting grading practices that allow for alternative assignments, extending deadlines, giving multiple opportunities, and allowing retakes. And while this flexibility can be challenging, it is also exciting because it makes sure that fewer students are left behind."

Megan Anderson Reilly
What Is Grace For?

CHENOA MEAGHER
2021 ESD 123
Regional Teacher of the Year

Sage Crest Elementary School
Kennewick School District

Crying and Chaos

My first day of kindergarten

For most, the first day of kindergarten is terrifying. For some, it might be a little less scary if you had been in school before and knew what to expect. For me, even though I had been in school before, it was definitely horrifying! I remember it like it was yesterday.

Before school even began my day was already in a downward spiral. All of the kids that were waiting in line were so noisy. It was so noisy! I just stared at the door, petrified with fear. It seemed as if most of the kids had never even seen a line before. They were playing around, shouting and not listening to their parents. As I continued to look at the classroom door that now looked bigger than life, I was able to block out some of the chaos around me, if only for a moment. The calm before the storm of my first day of kindergarten.

Finally, the bell rang.

As the kids entered the classroom, chaos ensued. Some

Inspirational stories from Washington's classrooms, featuring the Teachers, Principals, and Classified School Employees of the Year

47

started running and others were crying. I was on the verge of tears, but I knew I should be brave. Parents were not allowed inside — I was on my own, my safety blanket was gone. There were a few adults in the classroom trying to help calm the chaos. Finally, the class was quieted to a dull roar. We were all sitting on the rug and singing songs. This was awful for me because I hated singing, but the rest of the class seemed to enjoy it, so as long as they were occupied, I could tolerate some singing.

After what seemed like hours of singing, it was time to make a lunch choice and go to specials. As the directions were being explained, everyone started talking and some even got up and started walking around. Most of the kids weren't listening and no one had any idea what to do. No matter how many times it was explained, no one got it. The entire room was talking again, some were crying (I was one of them), and no one was making a lunch choice. One boy jumped off the chair then ran in circles shouting "spaghetti!" Others started to join him. The room was chaos once again.

This is a little peek into my first day as a kindergarten teacher. Crying and chaos was the tone for months to come. You see, I had taught third grade for thirteen years before I decided to make the leap to kindergarten. I considered a lot of things before I applied for the kindergarten position, but my sanity wasn't one of them.

How did I get here? I had the most amazing teaching partner in the world. She was the peanut butter to my jelly. We had taught third grade together for years when she decided to take a kindergarten opening in our school. I was so sad to see her go, but so comfortable in third grade. It was my happy place. About a week later, there was another kindergarten opening. What would I do? You already know the ending to the story. I took the kindergarten position. "They are 5 years old," I thought. What could be so bad?

It was not the kids that were bad, it was my preparation. Those who know me can attest that I am ALWAYS prepared. That's why this was so hard for me. I researched, read, and prepared the curriculum. I had weeks of activities organized and ready to go. Copies were labeled, filed, and alphabetized. Supplies were color coded and neatly placed on tables. The classroom was tidy from top to bottom. Until that first day — then my best-laid plans were running around in circles yelling "spaghetti!"

I have no idea how I made it through the first day. There were so many tears, most of them mine. What had I done? How could I survive 179 more days of this? I am going to be very honest: it was not easy. There was a lot of crying, regret, anger, and so much self-doubt. When I finally figured it out, when that little light went off, it changed everything. Some of my best thinking happens in the middle of the night. I was up, once again, agonizing over what the following day had in store for me (and going over my lessons), when it hit me! I not only had to teach them academics, I also had to teach them everything else: how to sit, how to line up, how to follow directions and stay on task — the "soft skills." This may sound obvious to you, but to me, with all of the academic pressures of a new grade level, it was far from my mind: I had tunnel vision.

Inspirational stories from Washington's classrooms, featuring the Teachers, Principals, and Classified School Employees of the Year

49

After months of chaos, we started over. It was baby steps for all of us, especially me. Most of my students had never been in school before and I had never taught kindergarten before so, we would learn together. Two months into the school year and I finally figured out that what I needed to teach them wasn't written in any teacher's manual. Then how would I know what to teach?

I started at the beginning of the day. Maybe if we started each day not running in circles and shouting, it would set the tone for the rest of the day. I taught the kids how to line up outside before school and how to come in the door. This is not a fairy tale, so my class did not magically learn these skills. Many of them still ran in circles shouting (and I did too some days), but we learned together.

We added routines like how to sit at their tables, how to make lunch choices, how to walk down the hall, how to hold a pencil, and the ever-challenging how to use the restroom without making a mess to our arsenal of awesome "kindergartener-ness." Some days were better than others. Some mastered the routines quicker than others. I slowly learned how to teach the skills that aren't in a teacher's manual while focusing on letters, numbers, reading, writing, and science as well as social and emotional development.

The following year I was more prepared. I knew some of the most important things I had to teach couldn't be found in any teacher's manual. I started with the basics on the very first day of school — how to line up and walk in the door. Were there still tears? Yes, but not from me this time. From parents whose babies had reached another milestone —

going to kindergarten. Did some kids still run in circles and shout "spaghetti?" No, this year we had chicken nuggets on the first day. Like I said before: this isn't a fairy tale. This is a real classroom. Each year got better and better. I became more effective at determining the soft skills that each unique group of kids needed the most. Together, as a class, we walked through those skills. Sometimes running in circles, but most of the time walking confidently. I had found my happy place again.

Then, in 2020, COVID hit and the whole world was running in circles and shouting "spaghetti." I needed to start over once more. Teaching through Zoom, building routines and bonds over a computer screen; teaching the soft skills that are necessary for kindergarten-ness without being in the same room as the kids. How do you "read a room" you are not in? I went back to that very first year I taught kindergarten. How did I figure it out? I determined what they needed to start out their day successfully and I built from there. Obviously, they were not lining up and walking in the door. They were logging on, muting, and unmuting. Those were the skills they needed, so those are the skills I taught alongside letters, numbers, and social-emotional development. As remote learning progressed into hybrid learning and I finally got kids into my classroom, the soft skills they needed changed once again. This time, I knew exactly what to do.

Whether they are at home on Zoom, in school with a mask on, or it's a "normal" school year, kids have to learn not only academics, but also how to conduct themselves in a social setting. They have to learn how to sit in a chair and stay

Inspirational stories from Washington's classrooms, featuring the Teachers, Principals, and Classified School Employees of the Year

51

on task, how to walk in a line, and how to make a lunch choice. Without these skills, learning cannot and does not take place. You can't build a house without first laying the foundation. Kindergarten provides the foundation on which all learning in later grade levels is built. We teach kids not only skills, but how to learn and function in a school setting. Next time you hear "it's only kindergarten," please remember my story. Without kindergarten, there is no foundation, there are no routines. There is only crying and chaos, running in circles, and shouting "spaghetti."

JACKIE HENTGES
2021 North Central ESD 171
Regional Teacher of the Year

Brewster Middle School
Brewster School District

Hunting and Pecking

A teacher's early fixation on grades evolves into a practice centered on learning and intrinsic motivation

When I was in middle and high school, I had a very fixed mindset. I thought all that mattered were the grades. The importance of learning for the long term was not on my radar. I remember obsessing about having an A- or a B+ and doing the math to figure out what I would have to get on the next tests or assignments in order to get my grade back up to an A. Several of my classmates had similar grades, but they were never as stressed out as I was. The difference was they were learning the fundamentals and building on them, while I was memorizing, testing, and forgetting. I had no foundation to build on.

I took typing my sophomore or junior year at Mead High School. It fulfilled a business class requirement for graduation, and if we could type 30 words per minute with zero mistakes on the smooth-as-silk Olivetti we would

Inspirational stories from Washington's classrooms, featuring the Teachers, Principals, and Classified School Employees of the Year

53

earn an A. So I strove for 30 words per minute with zero mistakes, developing phenomenal far peripheral vision so I could look forward but still see the keys. What a waste of time! By employing this strategy I devalued the grade, the class, and myself. I never considered how important being a good typist — now keyboarder — would be. I have wasted so much time throughout my life hunting and pecking while I watch students' and colleagues' fingers flow over the keyboard like concert pianists. As a kid, I remember adults saying, "you're going to wish you had done... when you're older." My typing deficiency didn't hurt me until college. My mom was now 1,241 miles away and 2 days by mail if I read the paper to her over the phone and had her type and send it to me. Being an independent young person in need of funds, I decided to take my hunt and peck method on the entrepreneurial track. I typed papers for a dollar per page. Running headers and footnotes at 30 words per minute and zero mistakes, I knew I was robbing myself of free time, but what else was I supposed to do?

In high school I had been taught different study skills and the importance of graphic organizers. I paid little attention because we didn't need to show proficiency, and their use had no immediate impact on my grade. I did learn the importance of outlining and highlighting chapters of written material because that was graded. It also helped me study for the test, plus we could use our outlines on the tests. Good test scores led to good grades — even more motivation to take my time and do my best.

I was expected to come to college with a foundation of knowledge. I needed to be able to read, write, do math, think, problem solve, stay organized, and type so a beautiful structure could be built. Instead, my foundation was built with disintegrating rocks and crumbling mortar. I had all the skills I needed, but sparingly. I was a good reader but mostly survived on CliffsNotes. I could write but resubmitted a paper on arthroscopy I had written my sophomore year in high school several times for several different classes.

Building an outline and my desire to go to college to learn were the only materials structurally sound enough to rebuild my foundation for learning. I outlined and highlighted every chapter in every textbook, listened attentively to the professors, and took notes as I had been taught. I still wanted A's, but I knew because of the deficit I had come to college with I was going to have to work hard for those A's. It would be a challenge, but I could do it. I played some college sports, but between practice and my new-found passion to make up for lost time with my education I had to forego a social life. My lack of investing in my learning early in my education caused me to miss out on a pretty important part of college.

In the Master's in Teaching program at Whitworth we were told to come up with ultimate outcomes that we wanted for our students. As I reflected on my own experiences in school, I wanted to make sure my students knew that when it comes to education, it's the learning that counts. As a result, the ultimate outcome I had for my students was for them to become thoughtful learners and communicators. To me, thoughtful students would be kind and considerate of others. They would be able to ask questions and form answers — whether through written, spoken, or even

Inspirational stories from Washington's classrooms, featuring the Teachers, Principals, and Classified School Employees of the Year

55

body language. I wanted my students to be self-aware and advocate for themselves. I wanted them to learn how to learn.

Twenty-five years later and each class still seems to have a few kids with a fixed mindset. Some students come in thinking like I did, that school is about grades. The grade they have reflects who they are as a person. People with A's know more than people with other grades. Other kids believe the opposite. If they have D's or F's, they believe they cannot learn or are unworthy. Then there are those that believe that they can't do math or science or read because it's hereditary. They believe they're either so smart they deserve A's for walking in the door or so dumb they don't deserve anything higher than a D. I try to erase this type of thinking and instill in them the understanding that education is about the journey, not the destination. I remind them if they are willing to put in the time and really grapple with the concepts the grades will come—that they are building a foundation for all the rest of the learning in their lives. We want that foundation to be sturdy and able to support any structure they choose to build on it.

Wouldn't it be great if all students were intrinsically motivated? Even if they could earn an A by typing 30 words per minute with zero mistakes, they would challenge themselves to exceed the standard. They would think in every instance:

"I will try my best, and I will learn for the sake of learning."

"I will be better tomorrow than I was today."

"Everything I learn will benefit me in the future."

"I will be a better teacher, better parent, and better leader because I invested in my learning."

As educators, we have the ability and possibly the responsibility to create environments where this type of mindset is encouraged and nurtured.

Inspirational stories from Washington's classrooms, featuring the Teachers, Principals, and Classified School Employees of the Year

57

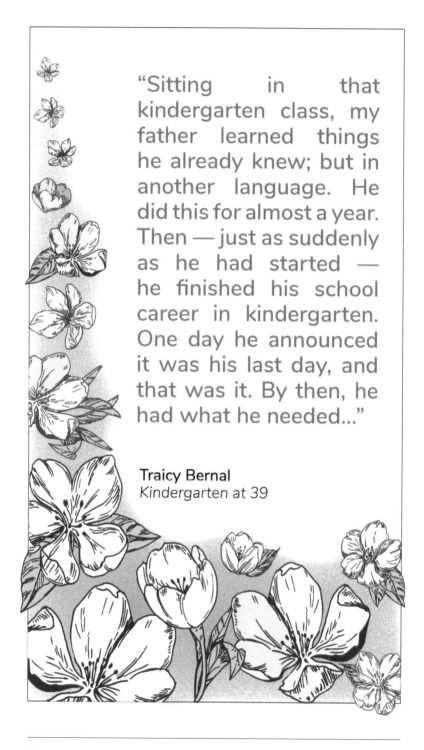

"Sitting in that kindergarten class, my father learned things he already knew; but in another language. He did this for almost a year. Then — just as suddenly as he had started — he finished his school career in kindergarten. One day he announced it was his last day, and that was it. By then, he had what he needed..."

Traicy Bernal
Kindergarten at 39

BEN BALLEW
*2021 Northwest ESD 189
Regional Teacher of the Year*

Arlington High School
Arlington Public Schools

(Not) Crying in Petco

A lesson in honesty

His name was Tommy. Not Tom, not Thomas, but Tommy. To compliment the name, he had carefully cultivated an aesthetic of antagonism: the flat-brim hat turned up defiantly, the shaggy hair flipped up just under the panels of the hat, and the low-slung backpack that never left his shoulders. Tommy was a legend before he entered my class, and he remained a legend long after he left.

I, on the other hand, was a first-year teacher with an empty classroom and an even emptier bag of tricks. But I was young and filled with all the hubris and righteousness of a rookie. Needless to say, I was not ready for Tommy.

One day during my planning period, I happened to look out of my window into the hallway. Frank Stallons, the math teacher across the hall, was talking to a student. Frank had always been something of an enigma to me: he exclusively wore bright, tropical shirts and cargo shorts to work, and

Inspirational stories from Washington's classrooms, featuring the Teachers, Principals, and Classified School Employees of the Year

59

his room was lined with toilet seat covers that his students had painted. His philosophy for teaching fell somewhere between Zen Buddhism and anarchy, and when he spoke, you often had the impression that he saw things as they truly were: nothing more, nothing less. On this particular day, he was speaking to a young man and I could see Frank asking him a question. The student paused, considered the question, and then burst into tears. Embarrassed, I turned away, but as I did, I saw Frank offer a quick hug and the two went back into the room.

I asked Frank about the exchange a few days later. He shrugged his shoulders, frowned, and said, "That young man was struggling in class the last few days, so I just pulled him outside and asked how he was doing. Turns out he was in a lot of pain, and I think he just wanted to talk. I think he should be OK now." He paused. "Sometimes we just need to be honest, you know?"

There's a performative element to teaching. Being a "dynamic" teacher means balancing your authentic self with a super version of yourself, one that is consistently the most optimistic, equanimous, and supportive human alive. This dynamic is baked into the profession: the first class in my teaching program was called The Dynamics of Teaching, and most of the assignments were pantomiming and performing skits or learning to use your body and voice to capture your audience. I grew up playing music and performing on stages, so I was so often concerned with my volume and body movement that I never considered the possibility of a quiet, honest moment between me and my students.

Nevertheless, I filed Frank's words away in my mind. In the meantime, Tommy's behavior in class began to escalate. Some days he walked into the class scanning the environment for potential victims, spending the 55 minutes insulting the people around him; other days he kept his head on his desk, waiting for me to make a comment and attack. During my first observation, he arrived 10 minutes late, looked at the Assistant Principal seated at my desk, and then swore at her and me before sitting down. She laughed to herself — she knew Tommy very well by this point — and I wrote up the referral, because what else could I even do?

By that point, I was despondent. Tommy's classmates were done as well, and one day one of them brought in a picture of him from middle school. Like any picture from middle school, it wasn't a good one, and somehow it ended up on the projector screen in front of the class. Tommy, arriving late as usual, was greeted by a chorus of his peers laughing at the picture. I took it down as quickly as I could, but I could see the damage was done by the look on his face. He spent the next twenty minutes picking apart his classmates and me with little comments, snorts, and crude words written on his papers. I think we all felt guilty about the picture, so we did our best to ignore his behaviors, but at one point it was too much. "You need to leave the room," I told him. "I will meet you in the hall, but you need to leave *now*."

This was it. I was done. I was going to put him in his place for me, the class, and the rest of the school. I quietly walked out into the hall and stood in front of him. I was shaking. Tommy's body was tense, his chin in the air poised for the fight we both knew was coming. I took a shallow,

Inspirational stories from Washington's classrooms, featuring the Teachers, Principals, and Classified School Employees of the Year

61

shaky breath and was about to speak when I glanced into Frank Stallons' window. He was teaching, arms flailing out of a garish, red shirt, and his students were laughing. "Sometimes we just need to be honest, you know?" I could hear him say. I dropped my shoulders, and turned back to Tommy. I knew nothing good was going to come from this exchange, and before I could think about it, I asked him, "Is everything OK, Tommy?" I could see his confusion. "What?" I repeated the question. "Yeah, I'm fine. Whatever. Yeah." I didn't know what to do after this or where to go, so I just repeated the question again: "Are you sure everything's OK? You don't seem like yourself today."

He cocked his head to the side, and he looked at me incredulously for a few moments. And then he burst into tears. I wasn't expecting this. Through the tears and snot, he explained that life at school and home was awful, and that he didn't know what to do. I was uncomfortable with the raw display of emotion, so I looked anywhere but at Tommy. I glanced into my classroom and watched as they stared back at us, jaws open in disbelief. I realized then that I had left the blinds open and the class had been watching the whole situation play out in real time. I clumsily moved so that Tommy didn't notice everyone watching, and I thanked him for being honest with me. I offered to help in any way I could, and, doubling down on Frank's advice, I offered a quick hug of support which Tommy declined. We walked back into class together. It was silent and remained so for the next 20 minutes until the bell rang.

Tommy didn't come to school the next day or the day after that. He showed up a few more times over several weeks, and then I got word that he had enrolled in a credit retrieval program offered by our local community college. I saw him a year later at a school concert. He flipped his chin up, smirked at me and said, "What's up, Ballew?" I stumbled awkwardly and said hello and that we missed having him around. But that was it, and I never saw him again around school or in town.

But our exchange in the hall never left me. It continued to haunt me in between periods and at night. Was Tommy's honesty a sign of trust or respect between us? Or had I just exposed a fragile young man to more unnecessary — and public — suffering? His honesty in that moment in the hall had unnerved me and left me unsettled. Worse, I never had the chance to follow up with him and get closure for either of us. As a result, I continued to avoid real honesty with my students and colleagues whenever possible.

Ten years later, my daughter and I are shopping for goldfish at Petco. As we round the fish tanks, I see a man walk in with his dog. We pass each other and I nod hello and he cocks his head to the side as if he recognizes me. As a veteran teacher, I know what comes next: this is a former student that I don't recognize and will awkwardly attempt to remember the name while talking to them. "Mr. Ballew?" he starts, and my daughter immediately runs off. "Yeah," I say, "let me get my kid and I'll catch up with you." As we make our second lap around the fish tanks, I see him again. I start to extend my hand with the perfunctory "Now, remind me of the name," but before I can open my mouth I know who it is.

Inspirational stories from Washington's classrooms, featuring the Teachers, Principals, and Classified School Employees of the Year

63

It's Tommy. I'm absolutely certain of it. He's wearing an outfit that looks straight out of my own closet, and his shaggy dog ("Winslow") is the mirror image of my family dog growing up. I don't know what it is, but something hits me like a freight train, and it takes everything I have not to burst into tears in the middle of Petco. I choke out the name, "Tommy!" He smiles, "Tom, actually, but yeah." I ask him how he's been, what he's up to now and everything in between. He tells me that he's been working in tech and living in Seattle for several years. He likes it, but he is thinking of moving back home — to Arlington. He pauses and chews on his thoughts for a second. "Hey, I know I wasn't easy to work with sometimes, but I want to say thank you. I have a lot of fond memories of your class."

I'm confused. What memories could he possibly be referring to? I want to call him on his bluff, because I don't have fond memories at all. I want to tell him that he's kept me awake at night for 10 years; I want to know if I've done irreparable emotional harm to him; I want to apologize for not being a better teacher, for not being there at the crucial moment. My daughter interrupts us and asks if she can pet his dog. He squats down to her level, tenderly hands her a treat and shows her how to get the dog to sit. She pets the dog and I tell her to say thank you. When they're done, he stands back up and looks me in the eye. "Thank you, Mr. Ballew. It was really good to see you." As I say thank you and goodbye, I know that we're both being honest, and something inside of me closes up and is whole.

The Indian yogi Sadhguru explains that relationships will never be absolute. Instead, a relationship is a variable, and you must conduct it right every day. You have to do your best, but sometimes your best is not enough. My experience with Tommy in the hall haunted me for so long because I wasn't being honest with him or myself. My best wasn't good enough at the time, and I couldn't see beyond my pride and insecurity to tell him that. One of the takeaways from living through a pandemic is that we can finally drop the pretense that we're "fine," that everything is "good" because, well, we're not and it's not.

Spending months separated by quarantine has deprived us of opportunities to connect and maintain relationships. Sharing and being honest with one another is one of the only ways we've been able to establish common ground and form communities. I've tried to be more honest with my students and colleagues lately, and I've seen improvements in these relationships: there's more respect, and there's more trust, and sometimes they even come back after graduation and we thank each other for those experiences. We don't remember the details, but we remember the honesty shared in those moments of conflict. Each day provides a new opportunity to build a relationship, to conduct that relationship right. Sometimes I'm not at my best, and in those cases, I always have Frank to remind me that, sometimes, we just need to be honest, you know?

Inspirational stories from Washington's classrooms, featuring the Teachers, Principals, and Classified School Employees of the Year

65

"Thoughtful students would be kind and considerate of others. They would be able to ask questions and form answers — whether through written, spoken, or even body language. I wanted my students to be self-aware and advocate for themselves. I wanted them to learn how to learn."

Jackie Hentges
Hunting and Pecking

YUBI MAMIYA
Student Contributor

Shorewood High School
Shoreline Public Schools

I Can Do This Too

Building changemakers through the power of representation

It was an interview article, the kind that usually showcases celebrities and famous athletes and the latest groundbreaking person captivating the world. Except, this article was about someone even more extraordinary: a Youth Ambassador of the Gates Foundation Discovery Center who was helping their community. As my eyes devoured the words on the page, I became more and more intrigued. Here was a girl of color (just like me!), who wanted to change the world (just like me!), and who was actually really truly changing the world (which back then, unfortunately, was not just like me). That rainy February evening in 8th grade was the first time that I had seen a young person's work spotlighted, and on the page of a *ParentMap* magazine no less! This moment sparked my journey of changemaking as I began to believe: "I can do this too."

My mentality hadn't always been so positive. During my early years of school, I moved from a neighborhood in California where the majority of people were people of color

Inspirational stories from Washington's classrooms, featuring the Teachers, Principals, and Classified School Employees of the Year

67

to a much whiter one in Washington. I immediately felt out of place.

Two parents who had recently immigrated from non–English-speaking countries? Check.

TV left the house when I was two years old and never returned? How bizarre.

First American citizen in my family? That's me.

I remember constantly being teased about my English fluency and inability to "be American" at school. Every time I was with my classmates, it felt as though I was sitting on a ticking time bomb ready to mark me as the outsider that I was. 3... 2... 1... cue the laughter of everyone but me. It didn't take long for me to become scared of sharing my voice. I was left feeling like I needed to prove myself in a never-ending race where I was constantly behind.

As I continued bouncing from public school to public school, I internalized a version of myself that was less than. Even when I saw other students receiving similar treatment from the education system, I accepted things as the way they were. American school staples like inaccessible opportunities, impossibly long waitlists, zero diverse role models, and lack of culturally encompassing curriculum became normal. I was so focused on proving myself at school by memorizing glorified versions of Christopher Columbus and all the old, white men who were groundbreaking scientists that I started to believe those were the only people who could ever do anything important. I was so determined to prove myself in the classroom — to prove that I belonged — that I forgot why I was learning in the first place.

The discovery in that *ParentMap* article that young people had the power to make a difference flipped everything for me. I started actively looking for places to carve out change, and in those places, I found some of the most empowering communities I will ever have the fortune of being a part of. I still remember my first testimony, which was on a Senate bill to help end human trafficking, in front of the Washington State Senate Law & Justice Committee. I had advocated for human trafficking support for the past year in the Dressember campaign.

I had written my testimony for hours with adults and my fellow council members at the Washington State Legislative Youth Advisory Council. I had rehearsed it over and over again at my host family's house the night before. Yet, when I slid into that seat, I was shaking. I had just listened to a few "experts" on the subject, and suddenly, all of my past insecurities had come rushing into place. Who wanted to listen to a little girl? If it hadn't been for the senator who thanked me for coming down to the capitol, my fellow councilmembers in the audience, and all of the supportive leaders who congratulated me, that memory wouldn't have been filled with as much conviction and inspiration as it holds for me today.

It is because of these people and experiences in my education that I continue to have the courage to make a difference. In the past few years, I've lobbied for equitable education legislation, helped to co-curate the "We The Future Exhibition" at the Gates Foundation Discovery Center,

Inspirational stories from Washington's classrooms, featuring the Teachers, Principals, and Classified School Employees of the Year

69

tutored disadvantaged and struggling students, learned from so many diverse and hardworking changemakers, founded neXt (my own nonprofit organization for education equity), and so much more. None of these would have been possible if it weren't for the wonderful role models and leaders in my life who gave me the priceless ability to be a changemaker.

I now know that the most important goal of the education system is to encourage students to be changemakers. It's been a rewarding journey, albeit one with many hurdles and pitfalls. I did end up becoming a Youth Ambassador at the Gates Foundation after all, just like the young leader I had first read about. I did a few of the things I've never dreamed I do and I'm still working towards a few more dreams of mine.

I do remember around a year ago — waiting in the hall of a library — when the December issue of ParentMap caught my eye. I had laughed inwardly to myself as I slid a copy off the stack and flipped open to a page. There were a lot of things that went through my head at that moment. Like how I really couldn't have picked a worse picture of myself. Like how surreal it was to see my name and the words "make a difference" in the same sentence. But when I look back at that moment, I still hope that there's a child out there who saw that article and thought to themselves:

"I can do this too."

MELITO RAMIREZ
*2020 Washington State Classified
School Employee of the Year*

Walla Walla High School
Walla Walla Public Schools

One Student at a Time

A knock at the door can change everything

I was born in Houston, Texas and raised in the Rio Grande Valley in South Texas. My parents were farm laborers, working in the fields and picking all sorts of different crops for all my young life. My sister and I were used to getting up early, around 4 a.m., and riding out to work with our parents to help with whatever we could at a very young age. I remember watching the sun come up in the morning and wishing I was still in my warm bed. As we got older, we were allowed to harvest our own rows of crops and that gave us a feeling of maturity and responsibility. It also motivated us to do a good job or we would go back to just helping mom. We took pride in that!

My parents divorced when I was about nine years old. My mother raised my sister and I alone from that point on. Times were very hard for my small family, and we worked very hard to just have some food on the table. Back then, resources were very limited and dependent on where you lived.

Inspirational stories from Washington's classrooms, featuring the Teachers, Principals, and Classified School Employees of the Year

71

The only work my mother knew was field work or working in packing houses, and she did that all her life. She only attended school up to the 5th grade, but she always instilled in us the importance of getting an education. My mother never learned to read, write, or speak English. She also never learned how to drive a car, so we always had to walk or ask people for rides to get around. By the time I turned 12, I was in the fields working with my mom every weekend and every summer to help pay bills and buy food.

At 14, I took it upon myself to write a letter to Kika de La Garza, Congressman of the 16th District of the State of Texas. I asked him for a recommendation letter in support of a special driver's license as I was the oldest in my family and we lived about 20 miles from the nearest town and, in case of a medical emergency, I could drive my family to town instead of calling for help. I was completely surprised when I received a response from him and that he supported my concern and gave me that recommendation letter along with his blessing. I passed both the written and the driving tests on first try and was given a special driver's license to drive at the age of 14.

From that point on, I would run the errands and even drive long distances. We were no longer dependent on others. Every spring, I would drive and we would migrate along with other families from Texas to Washington state. In late fall, we would make our way back to Texas. I left home at 16 but continued migrating with my family until the age of 19.

In my freshman year of high school, I dropped out with the intention of helping my mom earn some extra money. One day in particular, I stayed home because I was sick and did not go to work. It had been about 2 weeks since I had been to school. Suddenly, I heard a knock at my door. I opened the door and there stood a very tall, slim, white man with big boots, and a big cowboy hat. As I looked up to see his face, I realized that it was my history teacher Mr. Kirby. My mouth dropped open, and I thought to myself, "What in the world is he doing here?" In the poor part of town? In my neighborhood?

In retrospect, maybe that is what attracted me to the work that I find myself doing today. That moment when I realized that someone had taken time out of their day to check up on me, to see how I was doing. I still carry with me today the impact he made on me that day. The direct, honest, respectful way he talked to me is the same way I speak to all of my students.

I think that is the one thing that connects me to all my students and their families. They see me in their homes, visiting with their parents and families, sharing some food or drink, and having important conversations about how we at school can help them be successful.

Once you create that bond, the job becomes easy. You begin to build the relationship. It may take time, but once you have their respect and they know that they have someone in their life that they can count on, not much can stop that student from becoming who they want to be.

I will never forget Mr. Kirby saying, "Where have you been and what do you think you are doing?" It took me a bit to respond, as I was in some sort of shock, but I finally said,

Inspirational stories from Washington's classrooms, featuring the Teachers, Principals, and Classified School Employees of the Year

73

"Helping my mom work, but I am sick today."

He looked at me and said, "You are coming back to school. You will work for me on my farm after school and on weekends for a fair wage. After work, I will help you with your homework."

Over the last 40 years, I have thought of him often and have come to realize that moment is why I do what I do and why it comes so easy to me. So many connections made, so many lives that have crossed my path, so many great relationships, and so many great memories, and it all started with a knock at my door.

As a school staff member, a teacher, counselor, administrator, or classroom aide, we can be one of the most important parts of a student's young life. Our passion to support, encourage, and motivate can be infectious and inspiring to any student we connect with. We are the tutors, the enablers, and caregivers combined. We all can make a difference one student at a time.

TRAICY BERNAL
2020 ESD 112
*Regional Classified School
Employee of the Year*

Ogden Elementary School
Vancouver Public Schools

Kindergarten at 39

*An immigrant's quest to learn a new language
leads to going back to school*

f you have a desire to learn, you can. It is not every day that you see a grown man sitting in a kindergarten class, listening to a story and repeating after the teacher. But my father Sisinio Bernal had a passion to learn and improve himself. He was willing to do anything to learn English, even if it meant spending a couple of hours every day in a kindergarten class at my school. My father sang songs, practiced beginning sounds of each letter and number recognition, worked on shapes and colors, read many (many) preschool level books, and tried to be a part of classroom discussions among his five- and six-year-old classmates. I use his example every day to not only motivate myself, but as a way to keep his memory alive.

When I was ten years old, my parents and I emigrated to the United States as missionaries from the Republic of Panama. My father was a smart and extremely charismatic

Inspirational stories from Washington's classrooms, featuring the Teachers,
Principals, and Classified School Employees of the Year

75

man who captivated his audience every time he spoke with someone one-on-one or from the pulpit. His gift with words allowed him to connect with people in a very special way, but in his new country, he had to rely on my bilingual mother to interpret for him. After a year in the United States, he decided to take action and be creative in order to learn English.

Living in a small Kansas town of under 5,000 people in the mid-90s, English language learner classes were not something one could easily find, but my father was determined to learn the basics of speaking, reading, and writing. After a meeting with the principal of my small private school to brainstorm ideas on how to learn English an idea was sprung, and they decided he would join the kindergarten class for a couple hours a day.

Mrs. Judy Gannaway, Kindergarten teacher, remembers:

> I do not exactly remember how it came about, other than I knew he wanted to learn. I think he asked me if I thought what I was teaching the little children would help him and that started it all. Class with Sisinio happened right after school officially ended, but some days he would come in and work with me and the children. The children loved to have him there participating, talking with him, and having him be a part of reading. He was my student right under a year.

> Having his wife supporting him was a big help, and I imagine they were already working on some concepts at home. Being new and not knowing the language, having someone to help is big, because this ensures

they will be less likely to give up. In our town back then, coming across families new to the country was not common. People who set out to do something like what Sisinio did have to be determined to not give up after a while. Like anything you introduce yourself to, it takes time. It is like Jello: it takes time to jel.

Walking through the hallway with friends, feeling like I was less "the new girl from Panama" than I was the year before. I do recall feeling funny when we'd pass the kindergarten classroom and see him in the middle of the five-year-olds at circle time. Thinking it was something people from other countries do to learn English, my friends found it funny and different. I remember thinking my father was slightly odd for wanting to be in kindergarten.

In contrast, I did not struggle to learn the language. I had the advantage of attending bilingual private school when I lived in Panama, and my mother spoke English to me. Nonetheless, when we moved to the USA, I was still a beginner in the language. My first three months in this country were a summer of non-stop television with captions on and sitting at church trying to understand what people were saying. When fifth grade started in the fall, I listened, watched everyone around me, spoke only when absolutely necessary, and somehow was able to become an upper intermediate English speaker by the end of the year.

I have always called it a miracle, and it was, but as an educator I know the bits of English I had learned in Panama were connecting and my brain was finally being forced to use them. My father did not have a lot of English words

Inspirational stories from Washington's classrooms, featuring the Teachers, Principals, and Classified School Employees of the Year

77

floating around in his head. He was an adult who grew up in a monolingual world, and language acquisition is not as fluid for adults as it is for young children — one reason more US schools should have bilingual or immersion programs available for students. Our students are capable of so much more as adults if they are given the opportunity to learn another language at an early age.

Sitting in that kindergarten class, my father learned things he already knew; but in another language. He did this for almost a year. Then — just as suddenly as he had started — he finished his school career in kindergarten. One day he announced it was his last day, and that was it. By then, he had what he needed to move himself further up the ladder of English language acquisition. From a kind and welcoming teacher, he had felt included in that kindergarten class and gained both tools and confidence.

My father never did preach a full sermon without the help of an interpreter, but he was able to have conversations with friends, colleagues, and strangers. He could read and understand many books at various reading levels, and his English became stronger and more confident with each passing year. Although my father died when I was 17, I am confident he would have been able to preach without an interpreter by now.

When I reflect on my father's journey to learn English, compare it to mine, and now contrast it with my own daughter's journey to learn Spanish as a second language (instead of English) as second grader in an immersion program, I am in awe. Each one of us took a different path. One was traditional, one untraditional, and one (immersion program) which should become the norm. But in the end, each one required the same basic elements— the perseverance to learn despite any obstacles and family support and connections.

My father was supported as a member of my family (and through the never-ending encouragement of my mother), my early language development was supported by my mother speaking English with me, and my daughter is connected to Spanish language through her determined grandfather who instilled in me the importance of keeping your first language strong while also learning and strengthening a second language. I thank my father for allowing me to witness this perseverance first-hand. It not only continues to enrich my life, but also that of his granddaughter who learns the importance of hard work and drive from my many stories about his life. Let us all keep flaming the desire to learn well into our old age, no matter what may stand in our way.

Inspirational stories from Washington's classrooms, featuring the Teachers, Principals, and Classified School Employees of the Year

79

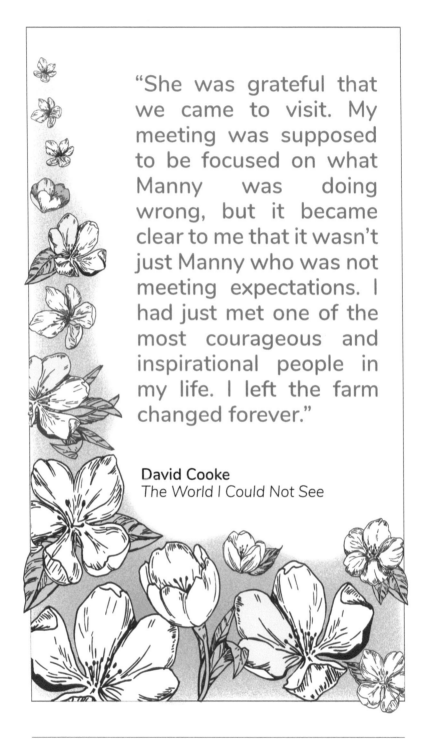

"She was grateful that we came to visit. My meeting was supposed to be focused on what Manny was doing wrong, but it became clear to me that it wasn't just Manny who was not meeting expectations. I had just met one of the most courageous and inspirational people in my life. I left the farm changed forever."

David Cooke
The World I Could Not See

JAELYN SOTELO
Student Contributor

Skyview High School
Vancouver Public Schools

Changemaker

How one student used her trauma to find her voice

As I've come closer to the end of my time as a high school student, just months shy of hitting one of life's most significant milestones, I've taken time to reflect. I won't hesitate to say that I am proud of myself, but maybe not for the reasons one would typically think. I've accomplished a lot over the past four years, but my personal growth and seeing myself flourish from one of the lowest times of my life has been by far the most invaluable and rewarding achievement yet.

When I was 14 years old, my father abandoned me and my mother. It was a striking blow to my self-esteem and self-worth, especially since we were so close. He was always the one who took me to my sports practices, helped me with my homework, and even served as advisor for our elementary school Math is Cool team. For a while, I grappled with myself because I couldn't understand why he had left. Were things really that bad? I blamed myself. What had I done that was so bad that he felt the need to leave behind his family and over a decade of memories that came with

Inspirational stories from Washington's classrooms, featuring the Teachers, Principals, and Classified School Employees of the Year

81

it? He had left at one of the most important times of my life — just months away from starting my freshman year of high school. For a while, I was simply a shell of my former self — an impostor of the person I used to be.

An important turning point in my journey was in November 2017 at the Washington State Prevention Summit in Yakima, Washington. In September, I had joined an organization in my community, known as Clark County STASHA. STASHA stands for Strong Teens Against Substance Hazards and Abuse, and we work to prevent drug and alcohol abuse amongst young people in our community using our own words and in our own way. I attended the summit with some of my fellow STASHA peer educators to learn about the skills and tools that we could take back to our communities to help lead the fight in prevention. At the summit, I was given the opportunity by one of the workshop hosts to write and share a poem about trauma. I took this moment to write about my father's departure — the one thing that had been causing me so much hurt and so much pain. I remember feeling reluctant as I strode up to the platform but overwhelmed by a sense of empowerment once I had a steady grip on the microphone.

I still don't know what it was, but there was a reason I felt that urge to put my vulnerability out there for everyone to see. I spoke about coming from a place of darkness. I spoke about the insecurities that plagued my thoughts. I spoke about the aching hurt I felt that left a void of emptiness. The more I spoke, the lighter I felt. When I was done, I felt as if an entire weight had been lifted off of my shoulders. I felt I was of letting go of everything my father had done to hurt me. I realized that this was my time. At that moment, I refused to wallow in my pity party of self-degradation any longer. I am bigger than my trauma. That day, I decided to take control of my destiny because my destiny led me to share my story and understand the power of my voice. I remember the feeling of determination to see where else it could take me.

That same feeling of empowerment and vulnerability that I felt when sharing my story in front of nearly 800 people has stuck with me to this day. The immense sense of passion I felt when sharing that poem about my deepest scars is what gave me the power to fight. It's been four years since I've spoken to my father. For a while, I let him define me. I let him consume my life. I thought my father took my voice when he left. As I've grown and learned throughout the years, I realized my trauma helped me find my voice. It has allowed me to be vulnerable and foster connections. My vulnerability has given me strength and allowed me to dedicate myself to others and my community. It has allowed me to shape my character to become someone that I am proud of. The day I decided to share my story is when I began to heal and take ownership of my voice.

I couldn't be more grateful for all the opportunities I've had and lessons I've learned over the past four years, both inside and outside the classroom. Being involved in my community has allowed me to help others and, all the while, find myself while on my own personal journey of healing. My community has helped me find connection, purpose, and passion. I have been able to host blood drives, speak with my representatives in the Washington State Legislature,

Inspirational stories from Washington's classrooms, featuring the Teachers, Principals, and Classified School Employees of the Year

83

lead other students in workshops on finding their voice, and so much more. I wouldn't have ever believed you if you had told all this to the person I was at the beginning of my freshman year of high school. I've learned so much about becoming a changemaker, and I've been able to see those changes reflected in myself.

KATIE LEE
2020 Olympic Region ESD 114
Regional Classified School
Employee of the Year

Vinland Elementary School
North Kitsap School District

Determined to Win

A love of music, determination, and family support were the keys to unlocking the learning of one student

P aul is a track and field star. His events are 50 meters and javelin. I have watched him become a champion and a star in so many ways.

Paul is sweet, funny, a little mischievous, and stubborn. He loves music, and it is one of his favorite ways to communicate — singing back to you. Paul's family speaks Spanish and is learning English. They are encouraging and supportive of Paul even when it is tough.

These are the things I have learned about Paul since I met him five years ago. But when Paul entered our program, it seemed like he had very few skills. He could not use the toilet or eat solid foods, and he was nonverbal. Paul has Down's syndrome. There are a lot of life skills he needs extra support to develop.

Inspirational stories from Washington's classrooms, featuring the Teachers, Principals, and Classified School Employees of the Year

85

When I met Paul, his diet consisted of Ensure in a bottle, yogurt, and tomato soup. So we started introducing texture into his food with the help of a food nutritionist. We would put crackers in his soup or fruit chunks in his yogurt. Eventually, even meat and veggies were added to his soup. The moment that Paul started to feed himself was empowering. He finally had a little independence. It was a big step that improved the quality of life for him and his family.

We started to increase Paul's vocabulary and the clarity of his words. Most new words came from his love of singing and music. We introduced communication in multiple languages: Spanish, English, and Sign Language. We used PODD (Pragmatic Organization Dynamic Display — normally a book or device that consists of symbols and words to support communication between people with complex communication needs and their communication partners) and PECS (Picture Exchange Communication System to help nonverbal or students with autism to convey their thoughts and needs). We realized that Paul learned best through music. The more we sang to him, the more he would sing back. We took him to music class, and he really started to shine. The music instructor allowed Paul to explore. He learned to strum a guitar, and he knew when to strum. He learned to play the glockenspiel and xylophone, and he was becoming good at it. When Paul had music in his life, he started to express his needs. He started to interact with his peers more and more. His peers were so open to his needs and presence. Paul was starting to grow leaps and bounds.

When he was in 3rd grade, I told Paul's family that he was old enough to join our Special Olympics Team. This would be an opportunity to meet new children and learn to be part of a team. His family was a little hesitant to sign up. They were worried that he would not be able to follow the instructions and participate in the program. Still, they did sign Paul up for the Special Olympics. Some days Paul would start running the track and field with his teammates, and shortly make a beeline back to his family. Mom and Dad would have to walk with him sometimes. They were not sure if they should continue bringing him to practice.

It was hard work. We started practicing at school on our playground track. Each day, Paul built stamina and increased his walking around the track. We also practiced throwing. Paul had a good arm, enjoyed throwing things, and could throw well. Running or walking in his lane was a challenge at first, but by the end of the season, Paul was able to walk the 50 meter. In 4th grade he was quickly becoming a track and field star. Everyone was proud of Paul and his accomplishments. More importantly, he was proud of himself.

In 5th grade Paul celebrated an important win. From start to finish he could independently use the restroom, leave the bathroom fully dressed, and wash his hands.

In spring 2020, when the COVID-19 pandemic broke out and schools closed, I thought, "Oh no, I hope Paul doesn't regress." I reached out to his family throughout the summer. They were also nervous about how to support Paul's continued growth through this pandemic. What might it

Inspirational stories from Washington's classrooms, featuring the Teachers, Principals, and Classified School Employees of the Year

87

look like? We were all asking these questions. We talked about some of the communication and other strategies that we used in class. His mother told me Paul was helping at the farm where his father worked. She said that he was helping with the farm chores, feeding the animals, and even driving a tractor. She expressed that she was a little envious of their relationship. She wanted to bond the same way. I encouraged her to allow him to help with her house chores. Paul was capable of helping sort socks, empty the silverware, or stir the ingredients for the evening meal. The family appreciated the support.

This fall, my supervisor informed me that Paul had not regressed over the summer. He was meeting expectations and is continuing to master his goals. Paul's new independence is a blessing to his family, and I am so happy to be part of his success.

Winning is different for everyone. From taking first place in an event to learning a skill for improving the quality of life — both are meaningful. Knowing what winning looks like for a student means really getting to know that student and what they are good at. Relationships like that take time to build, and that's why I spent time with Paul in preschool before he entered our program. We were working on the foundation for building a relationship. When we build that relationship and allow students to feel safe and loved, true learning begins. And when we start to open up and engage like that, we are all winners.

JOBIE FLINT
*2020 Washington State
Assistant Principal of the Year*

Cedar Heights Middle School
South Kitsap School District

Ebb and Flow

The changing shoreline of an educator

I often think about how the movie "Castaway" is like my journey as an educator. Truly, I never wanted to be a teacher and certainly never thought about being an assistant principal.

Ask anyone who knew the younger me. They will all tell you I was going to be a doctor. Growing up I spent many hours in hospitals and doctors' offices with my family as my father fought leukemia. Maybe that is what prompted my desire to be a doctor? In any case, I went to the University of Washington earned my Bachelor of Science in Microbiology, applied to a Ph.D. program, began my study focusing on recombinant DNA, and was miserable. Going to school and work each day was draining. Rather than being excited that I was doing my life's work, I felt that I had been sentenced to a prison in the shape of a research laboratory.

But, you never know what the tide will bring in and one day it brought me an opportunity. My good friend, who had

Inspirational stories from Washington's classrooms, featuring the Teachers, Principals, and Classified School Employees of the Year

89

grown weary of watching me be miserable, asked me why I didn't just do something else. Something else? She said she thought I would be a great science teacher as I loved science and clearly needed more people to work with. Thus, began my journey to today. I earned my Master's in Teaching from Seattle University and started teaching science in 1992. The tide had brought me my purpose, my passion. I love everything about teaching, but what I have loved most is the time spent engaging with my students.

Over the years, it is not the policies and the curriculum adoptions I remember. It is the students. The stories we built together of struggle and success. Donovan was a high school student in my biology class. Donovan had moved from foster home to foster home. He was currently living with another teacher in my building, and he was an angry young man. Each day I would make sure to greet him in the halls as he passed to other classes and each day when he came to my class be sure to tell him how happy I was to see him when he came to my class.

One day, he showed up halfway through the second period class, shaking, speechless, and with his fists balled up. One look at this young man, and I knew better than to start a conversation. I said, "You can use my back room to rest if you want." Donovan simply gave me a nod and headed to the back room. I quietly called the office and let them know that Donovan was with me and I would update them after class. At the end of class I went to the back room. Donovan was no longer shaking. I asked him if he could tell me what had happened. It turned out that in his second period class other students were talking about how foster kids must be really awful if no one wanted them, and he had overheard this conversation. He said he just got up and started walking. He first thought to go to his foster mom's class but he did not want to get her in trouble, so he came to my class. I asked him if was calm enough to go to the third period and if we could talk at lunch. He said he was, and he left.

Donovan did come back at lunch, and we worked out a plan for future issues. Over the rest of his time in high school, Donovan and I worked through many trouble spots. With the love and support of his foster mom and the assurance of refuge with me, Donovan gained some peace. I saw less and less of the angry Donovan and more of the happy Donovan. Donovan graduated high school and we remain in touch to this day. He is a wonderful stepfather to two lovely girls. The tide brought me the chance to teach more than science that day. It brought me an opportunity to teach self-control, problem-solving, and self-worth. It deposited joy and eroded arrogance. The relationships I built with students were as constant as the tide and a force just as strong.

Year after year, the ebb and flow of education marched on. So many students passed through my classroom, and our work together brought me more skills and tools as an educator As time passed, I realized that I wanted to work with educators.

As I enter my sixth year out of the classroom as an assistant principal, I draw on my experience with students and all that I learned from them to help me support, inspire, and grow staff. The tide brought me a new and amazing experience

Inspirational stories from Washington's classrooms, featuring the Teachers, Principals, and Classified School Employees of the Year

91

in administration. The things I remember most are not the district meetings or the policies and procedures I help craft but the time I spend engaging with my staff.

Mr. Rasmuson had one year of elementary experience and was in his second year of teaching as a middle school teacher in my building. He struggled with managing the class behavior, which is very common among new teachers and even some veteran teachers. I spent several hours a week in Mr. Rasumuson's room taking notes and providing support in real time. Mr. Rasmuson would visit me in my office, and we would talk strategies. We were working through a strategy for preparedness, and I shared what had worked for me and what I had seen work for other effective teachers. Mr. Rasmuson outlined his own strategy and explained why the strategies that I had explained just did not fit his style.

We agreed that he would try out his strategy, I would observe, and we would evaluate in three weeks. At the end of three weeks we met. Mr. Rasmuson said, "You knew that would be a disaster, didn't you?" I said that I did have my concerns and had addressed them via the examples we had talked about. Mr. Rasmuson laughed and said that it was like him working with his teenage son. Sometimes you have to let them figure it out but be there for support when all goes awry. Mr. Rasmuson still teaches with me and continues to grow and improve as a teacher.

So many changes have been etched in my coastline as an educator. Some years have been quite calm and tranquil and others a tempest of change. This last year has certainly been its own unique experience. Like the ever-changing coastline, at the end of this year we will have a new landscape of education. It will be drastically altered, but — I believe — improved. This constant change is one of the best parts of education. I get to see the continuous growth and development of both staff and students and use my time to discern their needs. I get to visit with those in my school and build the strong foundational relationships that lead to learning. While beautiful calm days are lovely. It is the wild days of high tides and crashing waves on the shoreline that excite me and bring me back. Each day I continue to wake passionate about my work — blessed by what the tide has brought me.

Inspirational stories from Washington's classrooms, featuring the Teachers, Principals, and Classified School Employees of the Year

93

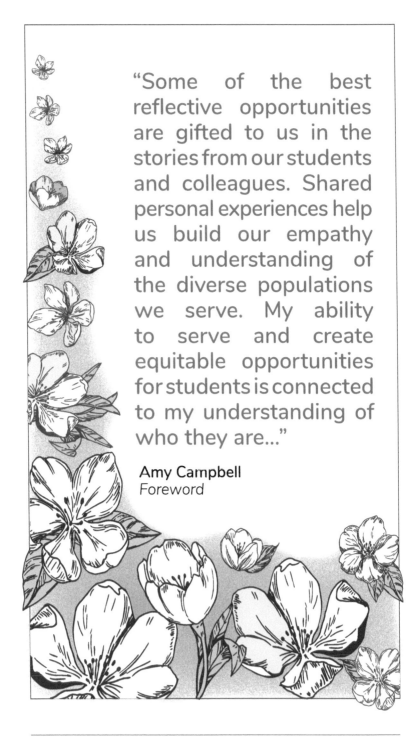

"Some of the best reflective opportunities are gifted to us in the stories from our students and colleagues. Shared personal experiences help us build our empathy and understanding of the diverse populations we serve. My ability to serve and create equitable opportunities for students is connected to my understanding of who they are..."

Amy Campbell
Foreword

ISAAC YI
Student Contributor

Glacier Peak High School
Snohomish School District

Reading Between the Lines
Failure is a great teacher

Most people may think America is all about success. I believe America is all about failing. As a second-generation Korean American, I have a unique perspective from which to view America. My parents traveled thousands of miles to pursue a future in a country that has achieved what their home country hasn't achieved. Many people in the world don't get the chance to fail, and I think we take it for granted. We learn more by failing once than by succeeding a thousand times.

Until sophomore year in high school, my English teachers would repeat the same line over and over like a proverb, "read between the lines." This frustrated me because whenever my teachers spoke those words, I could barely stop from saying, "I don't understand. How is this the author's hidden message?" They all mistook my lack of understanding for unwillingness to learn, despite my eagerness to do so.

When I walked into Ms. Browning's room that sophomore year, I was prepared to be ridiculed by the same proverb

Inspirational stories from Washington's classrooms, featuring the Teachers, Principals, and Classified School Employees of the Year

95

that my past English teachers had repeated countless times. But the most incredible thing happened to me. In the first weeks of school, she gave us an assignment to decipher the author's hidden message from a reading. I was clueless. I didn't understand what the author was trying to allude to. Was the author even conveying a message in the first place?

I approached my teacher during class with my paper, and I began to get nervous as she paced through my essay — frustrated because I knew that the answer was completely wrong. But when Ms. Browning looked down at my paper and read the sentences I wrote, she didn't ridicule or tease me. Instead, she leaned and quietly said, "come see me after school, and we can work through this together until you understand." I was doubtful, but I came in after class. She explained to me tirelessly the hidden details in the reading, the techniques employed by the author, and the countless mechanics of the author's purpose. I quickly became very frustrated when I didn't immediately understand. But when she soon realized that I didn't get it, she put down her pencil, looked me dead in my eyes, and said, "to succeed, you must be given a chance to fail." I am reminded each day of her voice telling me that I could succeed because I was allowed to fail.

Every day after school, she would sit down with me to explain and give hints about the reading material that we were assigned until I began to get more right than I got wrong. Before I knew it, the end of the semester came, and I had an A.

Her words will stay with me perpetually, because they truly defined my perspective on education. Whenever I fail, I always think back to that same classroom where I learned that failure is what breeds success. That is what Ms. Browning taught me, and it's something I try to adhere to every single day.

About the Award Programs

Since 1963, the Washington State Teacher of the Year program has selected one outstanding educator annually to serve as the Washington State Teacher of the Year. The Teacher of the Year is selected from a slate of up to 9 regional candidates representing Washington's nine Educational Service Districts (ESDs) and including Tribal Schools. In 1963, 1970, 2007, 2013, and 2018, the state program garnered national attention when Elmon Ousley of Bellevue School District, Johnnie T. Dennis of Walla Walla School District, Andrea Peterson of Granite Falls School District, Jeff Charbonneau of Zillah School District, and Mandy Manning of Spokane School District, respectively, were each selected as the National Teacher of the Year.

Washington began naming Classified School Employees of the Year in 2010. In 2019, Congress passed the first national recognition program for classified school employees. The Recognizing Inspiring School Employees (RISE) award is run by the US Department of Education. The Principal of the Year program is a project of the Association of Washington School Principals.

Anyone can nominate someone for Teacher, Classified School Employee, or Principal of the Year. Nominees complete a written application and enter the regional selection process. Each region recommends a regional finalist to the state program. The State Teacher, Classified School Employee, and Principal of the Year are selected from among these regional finalists by a committee made up of diverse educators, families, students, and education stakeholders.

Inspirational stories from Washington's classrooms, featuring the Teachers, Principals, and Classified School Employees of the Year

99

from seed to apple